VALANCY
AND THE NEW WORLD

D1248065

NANCY HOLMES

VALANCY
AND THE NEW WORLD

THE KALAMALKA NEW WRITERS SOCIETY

Canadian Cataloguing in Publication Data

Holmes, Nancy, 1959 -

Valancy And The New World

Poems

ISBN 0-969-3482-0-7

I. Title.

Book and cover design by Tarra-Graphics, Kelowna, B.C.

Cover photograph is author's grandmother, Dorothy Richards.

Photograph by Walter H. Calder, circa 1915.

Typesetting by Hart Publishing Services, Vernon, B.C.

Printed in Canada by Ehmann Printing Ltd., Kelowna, B.C.

Published by:

The Kalamalka New Writers Society
7000 College Way
Vernon, B.C. V1B 2N5

To my mother, Rosalie Holmes

I will stop here,
and watch the women
leaning out of the dark

ACKNOWLEDGEMENTS

A number of these poems have appeared in the following publications:

The Antigonish Review, Arc, Ariel, blue buffalo, Descant, Germination, Malahat Review, NeWest Review, The Prairie Journal of Canadian Literature, Watershed, West Coast Review, and anthologized in *Ride Off Any Horizon, Volume 2 (NeWest Press, Edmonton, 1987), Poets 88 (Quarry Press, Kingston, 1988).* Some of them have also been broadcast on CBC Radio, Alberta Anthology.

The author would like to thank the Alberta Foundation for the Literary Arts for a grant which enabled her to complete this book. Thanks to Christopher Wiseman, Joan Crate Taylor and John Lent who read and commented on all these poems. Special thanks, and love, to J. Leslie Bell, without whom most of these poems would never have been written, and who knows them best of all.

CONTENTS

PART I

The Broken River

Aunt Alberta, to save her dinner, plunged into an account of how a dog had bitten her recently and Uncle James, to back her up, asked where the dog had bitten her.

"Just a little below the Catholic church," said Aunt Alberta.

At that point Valancy laughed. Nobody else laughed. What was there to laugh at?

"Is that a vital part?" asked Valancy.

L.M. Montgomery,
The Blue Castle

Sunday Brunch: An Aubade

We come early.
The room is painted yellow and green;
the food lies pink and steaming
on lengths of cloth, white
like the cool flesh of blank pages.

At the table our eyes
are still hot and hands restless
from exploring the melons, the cream,
the platters of curled meat,
and gold sheaves of pastry.
Our knees touch in haste,
fingers peel oranges,
quickly
we slide slices of ham,
delicate baby scrolls,
into our mouths.
You reach for my plate, buttery
with eggs in hollandaise,
and the leather scent of you is there
between my teeth.
We are careless with the crusts,
the spills, the sweet waste of fruit,
the linen littered
and pages stained with excess.

More is impossible
but the end comes too soon
and regret settles slow inside me,
like a warm dark tongue—
when
you put this in my lap,
hard, closed. You whisper
I can have it at night when I'm alone.
I will open it and
all the fluttering white mouths
will take me.
All night, all night,
my hands in the book,
until the sky is gorged with dawn
and red.

The Disordered Lyric

and something that is perfect, that is not theirs,
　　　　　　　　like Mozart blooming
from the silver brain of the radio she gave him
a pure afternoon in the garret. His hand like hers—
　　　　　　　　　　　that slim

(could they write in the same room?) yet the stories
　　　　　　　　　　persist in the inky cord
of his typewriter. The haggard stack of books; to sleep
　　　　　　　　　　her heart slanted
into his chest, there held faster & faster was all
　　　　　　　　　she wanted

but oh, the emerald music plagues him.
"Just think of the Nazis." (romantic the French horn)
　　　　　　　　"Concertos in the camps
yet they burned books, didn't they? And your pale

　　　　　　　　　　Slavic skin
they would have," through the strings he whispers
　　　　　　　　　　on her breast
"beauty so distilled even the evil can love it."
It's so hard now. Hard to write with it. He won't
　　　　　　　　　get undressed.

Her bareness roughed against the yellow sun
　　　　　　　　drunk into his sweater
his fingers dream across the dull bones
　　　　　　　in her back. The music
suckling her skin, his lips. The clasp of symphony
　　　　　　　silken, unblemished

yet & yet—their mouths split open with the taste.
　　　　　　　Unbridled pomegranate
wet rush of red, burst of black seed & now &
　　　now　each panted word unfinished

Into the Halo

A black backbone
of rock
rakes the horizon
as if the earth were starved
and we could count
each jagged disc and knob
upon her brittle spine.

But
on the farm the earth is fat.
Gold slides of sun
shaft off the swelling clouds
and spill
onto the round brown backs
of horses,
shoulder-deep in wheat.
Bright bristles touch
sleek bellies.
Curving muscles ripple
in the yellow sweeping wheat.

All afternoon
the earth bones
lax and lengthen
under the
soft warm weight
of horse and wheat.

And what is the horizon but
the blind shot of black
that flashes
when we stare too long
into the sun.

Evol/ution

I. Beginnings

(Did the sea slip?
Or did she spit me out?

Dreaming of dolphins
dawn and you
I pant
beached and burnt-eyed.)

II. Coming Ashore

Warming breeds
with brittle snow
and sweats

(Tight bruised buds on trees,
red like my nipples you suck)

and mucous-clean mud smells
drip and diffuse
from earth's soft mouth.

III. Landed

Bristle.   Root.
Spread yellow flower flesh
—quick cactus bloom,
dark-dipped in night dew
wet as a kiss—
bright morning sweating pollen
sowing spores in our bed.

Riding Lesson

"the only exercise that uses the same muscles
as riding is sex"
he says sliding the whip down his thigh

the older women bounce and giggle
but the girl stiffens in her saddle
letting the trot jolt her hard

her fingers tangling with the reins
the wiry horsehair
her bridle hooked to his thin eyes

mother, mother, she panics

feeling only the fluid heat of muscle
between her legs, a sliver of metal
at her instep

thrust forward through the helpless air
turning towards him
coming to him at a gallop

he's smiling
fingering the whip

Not a Honeymoon

The beach singes the ocean.
We lie on stiff towels,
their softness burnt out of them.

The palms have a scaly thrust
and their fruit is hollow and hairy.
Our bodies bake in this heat without warmth.

In the end even lust is dry and yellowish
as you politely remove my hand
from your salted thigh.

Calgary Mirage

when we first came here we
bought a bed
a kitchen
and cooked visions

in the mornings
the mountains
crumbly pie crust
on the horizon
the glazed hills swirled and peaked
like soft meringue
the city boiled with people
bubbled with cars and buildings
like a glistening filling
erupting from
the sweet scoops of hill

mouthwatering potential

now my hands pick at the dry sheets
the kitchen windows are dark with grease

this is a high altitude desert
the wind panting at our roof
and drought crawling
into our lawn

Aquarium

I lug a ten gallon tank
around my middle.

People stare
as I slosh by
hoping to catch a flicker of fin,
a bubble,
but this skin-tight
aquarium is not on display.

Oxygen hums in and out
but even the tubes and motors are hidden.

I drape the tank with tablecloth
and feed the fish
apples through my mouth.

At night I feel
the ocean beat within me.
I dream of rolling water,
fronds of membrane,
pulsing coral

and soft, white starfish
unfolding in the dark.

Grace in a Cool June

the hearts of young violets
turn blue with cold

my fingers frozen
on the steering wheel as the car
thuds against
the small tender body of a bird

the peonies crack open
the baby's throat aches with crying
and in the house

light bulbs
hang grey and empty

fumbling with our clothes by a window

I watch the numb rain on the glass
wondering
as blessings twitch down

        white peelings of blossom

      clusters of robins, ripe and nervous

the sweet smooth heat of skin
in my hands

Tangle

it's a mess this history

a twist of sheets and skin
my hair in your toothbrush
our genes tangled in that small body

our marriage not one knot
but thousands

a visceral meshwork
no patient fingers
could unsnarl

the only possible extrication
now

a clean knife

Reading Sylvia Plath

Nightmares breed within her.

All night her limbs and throat lie cold
but her heart is heated,
her eyeballs lurch and tremble beneath her lids.

It's the gamble that excites her,
the intoxication of split collision,

the headless white horse
galloping into the fog,

the blind crow
flapping panicked in a sky
strung with sharp wire.

Each night she sates herself on
the teat of the succubus.

She swallows black pearls of milk
that lodge in her veins like cysts.

They decide to operate.

She's strapped onto a bed
that rocks and buckles.

She's locked up alone in a room so bright
even the shadows are white like X-rays.

Wide awake and
nauseous

she stares at the blank ceiling
and foresees a bloodied hole.

Static

in the alley on Tuesday morning
the scent of laundry
hangs in the air like wet sheets
cold sucks the dryer hollow

Wednesday, waiting inside, by the window,
for weather not too damp, not too icy

Thursday, the sky as hard as pavement
the walls of the house dent like putty

menace thickens in the future
a grey storm
crumbling with faulty connections

this year time stopped
for one moment
held us in her paper dry hands

   the baby in bed with us
   on Christmas morning
   our bodies a living cave
   his laughter like brooks and pigeons
   burrowing in our heat

   our fingers sparked
   when we touched him in the dark

In the Greenhouse

my hands beneath the angel's skirt
    bright shards
        break through my hair

gather the damp roots
    hurt and urgent in my palm
        air moist and plump
            wet body against my mouth

dig a thumbnail into bursting
    slice of stem

the delicate
    persistent splintering
        of water and glass
            my white bare back

tiny cuts surprise my skin
    the pink hook of bud
        my eyelid   up

        you
        in the hard glass column
        your slow hands
        fill the nanoseconds
        press the silent keys
        the terminal
        zero, one
        zero, one
        zero, one

Chinook

Sharp new moon,
sparrows' twitching flights
and melting snow.

How high the warming streams with west gold light
stretching a tip to touch the moon
strung out so slim and tight.

How thin the ice will be tonight.

Gothic North

I don't like this place.
Each time I breathe
a dead leaf catches in my throat.

And I think there's something in the lake.

I don't like this place.
The trees are dark and clotted.
They smell like coughdrops.
Webs, matted shadow,

there's even something in the lake,
a darkly hidden thing
rippling,
rippling

the surface
that just moments ago
was thin still glass.

There's too much water here,
cool green fingers
probing the black shore,

and there is something in the lake.
I can feel it.
The water fastens on my leg,
silver,
blank and
shuddering,
shuddering.

Lethe North

this is what I would find for you

    loose folds of snowy hill
    so you could sink slowly

    so snow would
    slide into your damaged mouth
    and fill you

    so you could stir your gently
    numbing arms
    to soften a pure hollow for your head

    so you could press your
    hot forehead against
    the safe ice,

    locked there

this is what I would find for you

if it weren't spring
and the buds weren't breaking
and bleeding
with sweet warm meat

Hunger North

Early spring
and all is starving.

Sun,
big butterball turkey
basting and sizzling
in its own grease.

Garden,
thick with peaty sauces
steaming.

Branches,
sticky syrup
seeps through
the tender twigs.

Spring,
oh time of famine.

I sink my teeth
into the seedy stew of earth
and fasten on the
wet red nipples
of young rhubarb.

Sour mother.
Sour feast.

Is this to be our fate in this bald land:
bitter cold usurped by bitter hunger?

Fractures

The dawn comes stiffly, chilled grey light congealing
on the shattered frost. You're tense in bed;
the baby's fists are tightened at his head—
the house is broken into rooms. A peeling
light is sliding, stale, off the ceiling.
The lamp is dimming like the bright anger that led
me to sleep by an ice-cracked window instead
of with you, in our bed, in the dark curve of healing.
Now you're awake. In separate corners we're staring
at walls waiting for rustling in the crib.
The sun ploughs through the frozen clouds. A sundog
splinters the cold and ice is bending, flaring.
You make room for me. I touch your hot ribs,
the rough quilt, and we slowly thaw and thaw.

Sunset on Clearwater Lake

stars snowing
  churn into ash

what's going wrong you ask me

watching the sun chewed by fire
    the sound of crumbling   dark
    and smooth like the
      ripple of the loon

where are we now you ask me

as gravity caves in
    embers thicken and dull

space bleeding dust
    and heavy white ash

I slide into the lake
  limp water cools my scalp

nothing floats anymore you tell me
    your tongue soft and flaking

it's a slow slow descent
    into ice

A Red, Red Rose

Driving home, the winter sun white and glittering,
the long, clean flower he gave her lying in her lap.

She stops at a red light in a construction zone.
Yellow loose machines drill the bitter pavement.

The limbs, the teeth barely under control,
jerked at the last icy moment into position.

Her lips are still warm with him and her hands
are cold and plain, just the wedding ring and pale diamond.

Her fingers snap the slender stalk of white carnation.
Damp scent seeps out from the naked petals in her lap.

Yseult at 100 KM/H

music from the late night radio
presses against the icy bulge
of windshield, against
her temples

where he's touched her
flecks of colour burn her skin,
flowers of warmth shift, stinging splashes
glisten beneath her coat

streets slide away under the headlights,
cold, empty and
terribly fast

driving into black sails

he is already asleep,
the dark sheets on his cool skin

there   home

the speed is all—
the lying, the going

either way it's ruin
her cold foot on the floor

The Vegetable Garden

"The garden is poisoned," she says.

We're walking the dog
through a dull field a block
from her new house.
The dog loves the smell
of small death
in the grass.

"Not even a weed.
I've tried everything."

We turn back into the dry wind,
hook the dog to the leash,
walk back to her house.

She's worried about her husband,
and the other man,
the lies she wants to tell.
Her hands are white and straining on the leash.

"Not even compost helps.
Nothing.   I'm going to give it up."

We come to her front yard
and I stare at the flower pots,
hot and mangled
geranium, pink guns of fuchsia,
and the corrosive hearts of marigold.

Comedies for the Fucked of Heart

Once a nymphomaniac
fell in love.
It was last December,
the city as grey as an ashtray.
With a forty-five year old man,
poor bitch.
She wore a red scarf around her neck
all winter.

Then there was the affair of the married woman,
eight months pregnant.
Cracked with lust, her belly
graceless and gorgeous
and terribly pale in
broad daylight,
her lover touched her
with averted fingers.

The frustration, the inflated
self-consciousness trying to make
art of it.
Art! The only art this one's
good for is the quiet fuck
against a wall
trying not to wake his mother
sleeping down the hall.

And we've both heard of the teenager
in the front seat of a
probably borrowed car
the green slits of the radio throbbing.
The dark grope for the zipper.
Afraid of it. The razored chill.

For their comfort,
let us praise
the desperate boredom
of lies.

Killing Adonis

Winter has scarred her eyes.
Soon she'll be as blind
as the snow on yesterday's hill.

Her fingers are dead with cold
and her feet frozen as she lies
by the bridge, alone in its shadow.

The river is broken,
ice caving in, ice
choking each bank and hollow.

She clutches the black box
and dreams of cold explosions
and of her heart.

their skin
melted away beneath her
touch   drenching
her   she still can't
believe it   always
she wanted to keep them
covered   but gone now
his hands in the blankets,
the soft dark down, the small heads

Not even the sun breathing on the cracked cement,
not the grass rising from the sheets of snow,
not the wild crocus

with   pale   translucent   stem

(oh, his long white thighs
before the blood)

not spring,
not this helpless, wasted
spring

can stop her now.

Thinking of Michelangelo

One cold afternoon in Florence
I touched the marble foot of David
and felt human heat.
I saw his naked ribs rise and fall,
his marble muscles slightly
bulge and flex.

I imagined
a male brute of a God
reaching a gnarled forefinger down
to fondle that bright body
into life.

Later, alone
in my hotel room,
paper seemed a cool and flimsy thing
and my hands were limp.

PART II

The Lost Eclipse

His cedar paddle, scented red,
He thrust down through the lily bed;

Cloaked in a golden pause he lay,
Locked in the arms of the placid bay.

Trembled alone his bark canoe
As shocks of bursting lilies flew

Isabella Valancy Crawford

Valancy and the New World

(for Isabella Valancy Crawford and L.M. Montgomery)

Nine loons in the bay,
she knows it is a sign
of fertility, eternity,
white and silver rings
looping the water forever.
She curls around her lover's body
as their laughter slips down the lake
like quick canoes.

The honeymoon in Europe
hurts her cool round vision,
the sun brilliant on old ruins.
Who ever thought stone could look so soft?
She meets a man, his voice
jewelled with history, places,
wars. Desire locks
the scent of cedar in her,
perfume in her throat so strong
she feels like a new-made box,
oiled,
the ax finished with her.

At home, the evergreens seem to heal.
They rug the valleys,
stitch the rifts,
and knit tight dank wool into sharp rock.
Her flesh grows moist and supple again
but age has penetrated her bones.
She feels how fast things grow old
though they be deathless.
The thick valleys bury her in their haste to seed,
thundering rivers drain away her skin like silt,
fraying cedars, drinking from the lake,
shed splinters.

39

In the cabin, under furs,
shadows crackling in the night,
she thinks of the man from Europe
and her organs dry out.
The hook of the new moon slices
through her brain and rises dripping.
Water lilies aren't sharp and silver, she thinks.
Water lilies are how his hands used to be,
white and tender on her skin
in their tent,
lilies on her thighs
and in her mouth,
the red, warm cedar paddle.
Married love, the moon:
endless circular silver
sliding in and out of dead wood.

You Search for History, I Read Jane Austen

You told me you almost found it
at Culloden
when you walked
through the cold breath of dead men
and your skin felt threatened.

I watch you reading in your chair.
Something in me loosens,
slides,
when you say you want me,
or when I wonder
about the baby we never mention,
or when you tell me other secrets.

The light around you is warm and yellow.
In those pages you're peeling back
layers of living bodies
to find it.
Sifting through the mothers
with dead boys,
throwing salt on the limbs of lovers.

You want to expose
the long black nerve of history,
and prod it
to make it move.

I think of the empty bed
in the other room
and my mouth silent on your skin.
I watch you reading
under the warm lamp.

How your eyes surprise me,
my fingers caught
in this white-throated book.

Victorian

when I was a girl I lay in bed
tucked the blankets around my waist
and made a crinoline in the dark

men, their thighs still warm from horses
would kiss me
my legs pillowed and covered

I never knew about Madeleine
arsenic in her petticoats

or Palmerston raping the ladies-in-waiting
at night in Buckingham Palace

or prostitutes torn in the fog

or the Queen uncontrollably pregnant

but sometimes I saw the word "burial"
so rich in those dark books
in the endless thick of paper
and their webbed handwriting
pinning brains in black lace
the novelists weeping
for dead children,
quiet now,
the way they liked them

later, all those young girls
Alice, and Alice's stockings

even now when I own a thousand books
and some silk underwear
how utterly lost
the century is to me

"Jennie E. McDonald, 20th Birthday, Aug. 26, 1898"

I have a photograph of her when she
was older, perhaps just before the War.
Her round chin and white ruffled collar, matronly.
Her eyelids tilted, full lips slightly apart,
hinting at a cumbersome passion. Her hair, dark coils,
(my father says it was red) as thick as this volume—
Whittier's Poetical Works—leather, gold foil
decayed. In these pages I see Victorian rooms,
cluttered columns of verse, her father's brick house,
Venetian goblets, silver, roses and china,
this book new, and lacy ink only hours
dry, her pencil pressing X's on lines:
    "Blue sea of the hills!—in my spirit I hear
    Thy waters, Gennesaret, chime on my ear."

At her age, at twenty, I was in the Klondike in August.
The trail from Skagway slit the forest and mushrooms
bloomed red until the black, choked rock of the Pass
rose dead and misted above me. So bare, and no roof
for miles, I shivered on that skeleton of hope:
two thousand pounds and lust through smothering ice,
all winter dragging passion up that slope.
Now, nothing but silence and lengths of paper faces.

Her dark X's on the page, buried
in quiet leather. Hunched bodies in the snow.
The deep, white layers of dream I want to blow
open, to touch the blood, erase obscuring
death, to catch them stumbling on those hills, and yet
this troubles me: that such desire's a wasted gift.

We Give Each Other Books We Used to Love

My hand runs down the length of shelf.
I used to read these each Sunday afternoon
so privately.
How flexible time is,
how like the pages of a book.

The white centres crack open, muslin
enfolds my fingers and covers the feeling
of your dark hair on my skin.

Anne is alone in her bedroom,
creamy tea-roses in her hair.
A sealed garden, green secrets growing
late in the crabbed and dying century.
Slender hands on a smooth railing,
the shadow of a tall man
glimpsed in the corridor below.

I know this was you.
Permanence can move backwards,
into time.

If I give this to you,
my hands will be as fresh and empty
as air around a scentless flower.

I trust you to peel off the white cotton,
wilted lace, damp ribbon,
unstring the hair.
Moist ties in your fingers,
knotted and torn at.

Then your warm hands inside,
reading the places
where memory doesn't work.

The Tobacconists

(for Leslie)

Even with the light out, I turn the pages.
The ragged scent of tobacco rises from the sheets
and I feel I am touching you while you are sleeping.

I dream two men look up as we walk in.
I'm holding your hand and wearing a skirt.
My cigarette is slim and dainty.

One cabinet is full of ornate cigar boxes, hinged open.
Rows of tobacco jars line an oak-panelled wall.
Black Robe, Virginia Rifle, Arcadia, Grosvenor, Cavendish.

He studied pipe and cigar ash, one hundred forty types.
Most men smoked then, even waiting in a wood to commit murder.
"Such an ash is only made by a Trichinopoly."

In my room there are flakes of tobacco under the bed,
in corners, mixed with dust now
but he'd find them easily.

Hooves clatter on the cobbled street. A cab draws up.
Hurried feet on the seventeen steps, the door bursts open,
a distraught woman rushes in, dressed in black.

"I would not tell them too much," Holmes said. *"Women
are never entirely to be trusted—not the best of them."*
Tonight I imagine you were silent. Restless, smoking.

The bullet holes in the wall, the files on the chair,
the scattered books, gas lamps, and smoke
thick around his head.

The long ashy fingers carefully pack
wine-coloured leaves into the bowl.
The match flares.

*"Beyond the fact that she is in mourning for a parent,
has two children, is a typist who has come down in the world,
has dressed in a hurry and lives in Coburg Square,
I can tell you nothing."*

In the dark clouded room, suddenly my heart is afraid
of the next revelation, knowing the weakness in my story,
as you turn and turn in my sleep.

Eminent Florence Nightingale

she returned incognito

in a few years
everyone thought she was dead

but she could charm
gangrene off a man

she lay on her couch for years
her head, a mathematical storm

when she moved to a new house in London
she hired two huge wagons
to cart her statistics
on sanitation in India

she wrote a treatise on sinks
ran the War Office
briefed every Viceroy of India

her anniversary had nothing
to do with the Crimea
August 2: Sidney Herbert's death
because she killed him
with overwork

though ninety years in bed
she slept only with paper

I love to watch Strachey
undress her
a nurse stripping a patient
his elegant
needles
as pure
as her

her brain, his story
the best part of her

though this, too, is a lie

The Laureate Recollects

(for Randy Miller)

Now that he is old and not working
he dreams of the garage at Grasmere.
Not as it was,
not the sick headaches,
warm rum and water,
long, wet walks for letters,
and Dorothy nursing him on the carpet,

but rather the work.
His stained fingers
wiring the white skin of the page,
his brain hard with rows of wrenches,
the bolts oily and solid on the table.
When rain drenched the windows
his hands moved deep engine rhythms
into blank metal and cold walls,
and Dorothy was in another room,
writing away for parts.

Now he drives alone in his old Mercedes
over Westminster Bridge. It's early morning
and the endless walls of London glisten
across the windshield.
His heart stills with great indifference.

Years ago his best friend choked
on bankruptcy
and Dorothy gave up,
disappointed by lack of response.

In vain
he remembers
the garage at Grasmere:

three silent cars coming apart in the grass,
and warm ink leaking slowly
into the soft, grey lake.

Where Did You Go, Lord Elgin?

Two hundred years ago
the young Scottish lord
brought Galatea to London
with teams of white horses and chariots.
He gave her his name and a cold mansion
where she lives today without him.
Does history confuse her?

Like thinking of you long before we met
working the quiet Archives of the Glenbow Museum
married to someone else.
The young Indians
with black braids and mirror sunglasses
asked you for old treaties
and other Blackfoot documents
and you spoke to them in a Scot's English.

I was fifteen, then,
emigrations sifting through me, unnoticed.
I went alone to visit the Acropolis.
There into the gaping white marble
I was thrown, spinning. This is it—
never being the first one
and how everyone leaves.

Later in a taxi,
the Parthenon far behind,
the Greek driver steers with one hand
until suddenly all the church bells
in the city start ringing.
He lets go of the wheel,
crosses himself
again and again.
We swing through the traffic circle
helpless.
Oh Lord
Elgin lost
now my lover
touches me without a country
my heart travelling
and baffled
with them.

And now, still spinning.
There are bare ivory muscles
in cold countries.
Crack the prairie open
and find black, foreign ice.
Two slender flowers grow
in the ancient woods
beneath the great ruins.
It is Athens, London,
and all the other deep white territories
without borders
that we turn to
again and again.

The Duke of Wellington Discusses Macaulay
With the Queen

"Publish and be damned."
— The Duke of Wellington on the occasion
of attempted blackmail by Harriette Wilson

(Harriette's mother was a stocking-mender.
A good living then,
trousers for men not being common
until 1820.)

"Admirable Horatius! So gallant and heroic!"
The Queen in her fervent ribbons.

(By now Harriette's profession, too,
is obsolete.
She did make a career change in middle-age:
novels, memoirs, *romans à clef*,
and she married.
But once she kept Wellington
waiting outside in the rain
while she finished off another lover.)

"Bows and arrows, m'am.
A smart volley with bows and arrows
would have stopped the Three."

(Harriette, too, knew
his contempt for literature
was perfect.)

The Marriage of Reverend Charles Kingsley

Hear me, I would touch you.
Don't say you're tired; this is marriage.
We've been so long apart, so long
since I tied your one white wrist
to this stalk of wood
on our bed,
drew back the thick curtains
to see the gleaming moon rising
on your pillows and your flesh
like bread waiting in the dark.

This scent is worse than hunger.
It excites me how we have spilled memory
that warmest water
into these sheets, this floor,
rubbed it into that wall,
and over the stile in the meadow
or in the leather study below—
my hand laying down the book,
the Armada flaunting its white in your skirts.

Stay now, they are the children of our marriage.
I took that small key of curled hair
with me to the Alps, and to German universities.
Your scripture fills my mouth, always.
I am the chaplain at the black court.
Let me sermonize you.

For our wedding I drew you a sacred picture.
Our two bodies unclothed straddling the Cross,
one wrist tied, the other hand searching
God Almighty
searching you my sainted
ah Fanny, tell me you feel this
this holy plunge of love
this one red nail
through our hearts.

Mabel Loomis Todd

"Emily is called in Amherst the 'myth'. She has not been out of her house for fifteen years... She writes the strangest poems, and very remarkable ones. She is in many respects a genius. She wears always white, and has her hair arranged as was the fashion fifteen years ago when she went into retirement. She wanted me to come and sing to her, but she would not see me. She has frequently sent me flowers and poems, and we have a very pleasant friendship in that way. So last Sunday I went over there with Mr. (Austin) Dickinson. Miss Vinnie, the other sister, who does occasionally go out, told me that if I had been otherwise than a very agreeable person she would have been dreadfully tired of my name even, for she says all the members of her brother's family have so raved about me that ordinarily she would hate the sound of Mrs. Todd."

Mabel Loomis Todd's Journal,
September 14, 1882

The evening after this visit to Emily Dickinson, Austin Dickinson *(Emily's brother) and Mabel Loomis Todd declared their love for each other, and over the next thirteen years conducted a passionate affair in the heart of nineteenth century New England. They frequently met behind the closed doors of the dining room in Emily and Vinnie Dickinson's house. Austin lived next door to his sisters with his wife and three children and Mabel was married to David Todd, professor of astronomy at Amherst College. In 1886, after Emily Dickinson's death revealed over a thousand poems hidden in a drawer in her bedroom, Vinnie Dickinson asked Mabel Loomis Todd to prepare the poems for publication. Mrs. Todd edited and published many poems, which otherwise might have gone unrecognized, and then located and published the poet's letters. In this century, her daughter, Millicent Todd Bingham, continued the work. In 1955, the* **Complete Poems of Emily Dickinson** *was finally published in three volumes, edited by Thomas Johnson.*

Mabel Loomis Todd

I. In Emily Dickinson's House

One day Emily sent
a poem into her
on a silver tray.
Alone with A.
locked in the dining room,
his wife next door,
the tray cool in her hands,
she slid between
the deceptive satin
of the dining room table
and his beard.
How she held onto the tray.
How his hands ran like rebels
in her clothing
and she loved it.
How the pearls rolled down her thigh
and collected on the tray.
A. for adultery,
this is New England.
Give me a century and I will read you,
too, in my hands.
How love becomes devotion
to skin and ghosts.

For some years she did this everyday
—mouthful by
mouthful—
with A. and later at night
go home for David, too.
This is a woman poet.
Each dash
a scent
of the whole.
How we need the image of
her skirt around his throat.
If we could only get enough.
How we fall hard on
the slant of love.

III. Millicent Todd Bingham

Her mother wore A.'s ring on her left hand,
moved David's to her right.
The young daughter watched
every gesture as
she grew up,
wrung
by the inheritance.
She kept all the paper,
the coded diary
with "A." "A." "A."
stitched into the white page,
herself a small round footnote
and the poems taking more
and more
space.

IV. The White Dress

The silver tray,
a wedding present.
But who is the bride in a marriage?
Does she wear the warm length of his skin
or is she the white gown
hanging on the hook of him?
At the wedding supper
in the dining room
her ghost moves from chair to chair.
Her unseen small hands
serving slivers of loss.

V. Amherst in Alberta

On her way to Japan
to photograph a total eclipse of the sun,
her train was delayed in Canmore, Alberta.
Her eyes telescoped inward
dark brown glistening along the stream
of Milky Way to the dining room table in Amherst.

This is my country.
I drive high into the west
past Canmore into the breaking forest.
I think of how the ship
didn't leave without her,
how the sea warmed and foamed
beneath her feet as she went further
on the arm of her disappointed husband.

She wrote a love letter in Alberta.
"Austin, oh my true husband,
the mountains burst through the dormant forest
all raw. They make me
ache for you. Remember that last afternoon
in your sister's house?
How we parted."

She was the first white woman
to scale Mount Fuji
but the bridal mists she brought with her
obscured the sky.
The eclipse was lost.

Emily enclosed upstairs writing the poems.
Austin reading the letter months later
in the dining room,
his wife next door.
The white page heaving with a continent
and the great lapse of time.

How geography spreads
into this century.
I inhabit her passionate body
the white dress
around the mountains.
Writing of an expedition taken and failed,
writing, writing
of the snow falling in my country.

The Last Biography

Julia Duckworth was the niece of the great Victorian photographer, Julia Margaret Cameron. Julia Duckworth's second husband was Leslie Stephen, the editor of **The National Directory of Biography.** *Their daughter was Virginia Woolf.*

A Photograph of Julia Duckworth
by Julia Margaret Cameron

I. I am startled by the descent.
This woman's narrow face
leans out of the dark,
slides close to me.
She is as familiar as my grandmother
who died
before I was born.
I know her through photographs,
eyelids weak with grief.
I've seen her a hundred times
imprinted on her daughter's
twentieth century face.

Inheritance is not always the issue
nor blood unless it shows up black
in a story.
I feel the half-dark of Cameron's art
impressing my brain. Darkness
belongs and persists in her photographs
as her camera embeds white cloth,
bare skin, loose hair
into shadow.

I see now
black and white
is the most seductive connection.

II.   Lips, eyelids, cupped hands, and parted hair.
The ardent hair of Magdalenes and angels
and the vigourous beards of the old men she loved
like fathers, warm gods in waistcoats.
Tennyson, beloved patriarch and neighbour.
They shared books on art and religion.
She took him over and over:
monk, prophet, saint, in robes.
Her hands in the dark cloth,
the beard curling under her eyes.

She dressed her servants and nieces
as Madonnas in crinolines and bedsheets,
with white babies in their laps.
She learnt techniques for posing
naked children
from Lewis Carrol.

Hands in the dark cloth
moving the light underneath.
In the dark tunnels even now
I can feel the crisp and electric hair.

Hair dazzles her with its net
of light and dark.
Auburn hair that fires under lilies.
Men with huge springing beards.
Darwin's ape-like forehead.
Carlyle bristling, Browning's elegant trimmed chin,
and Tennyson again, ageing so beautifully.

The camera swelling them
in silver wash.
She touches the wet satin of negatives.

The widow's skin starves
under the black cloth
and her hair aches
in a triangular mane, uncombed.

III. The stories expand helplessly,
pile up even as darkness shuts out more and more.
The white faces of the pictures wear thin.
I see the threads
married, torn, passed on down
the length of a century
twisting uneasily in the dark cloth.

Her face staring into my own.

I go down like Alice,
down a shaft
of light
from her camera.
Julia Margaret's niece,
Julia,
married Leslie
and their daughter Virginia
was once engaged
to Strachey
whose glittering pen
opened the cool, black body
of her father.

I'm lost in this garden
of black and white.
The shutters of the house
are only half-open.
In heat,
it's summer,
bush and hair burn
on the blurred lens.
How virtue pants
and loosens her clothes.

I will stop here,
and watch the women
leaning out of the dark,
watch them parting
the thick, white sheets
of paper.
I will stop here
and lean on the window sill,
watch for awhile
and mind the time.

Diadems—drop—and Doges—surrender—
Soundless as dots—on a Disc of Snow—

Emily Dickinson

THE KALAMALKA NEW WRITERS SERIES

The Kalamalka New Writers Society is proud to introduce Nancy Holmes of Calgary, Alberta as their first national competition winner. Her manuscript was selected from a slate of fifty-three entries from across the country.

With the completion of this contest, we would like to acknowledge the work of the five judges: David Arnason, Don McKay, Glen Sorestad, Tom Wayman, and Christopher Wiseman who donated their time so generously.

Our appreciation goes to Whitney Buggey, Director, and Ken Hewson, Assistant Director of Okanagan College, Kalamalka Centre, for their moral support, guidance, and faith in our project.

Special thanks goes to Tarra-Graphics who designed the book and saw to the scheduling of each phase of publication.

For further information regarding the competitions or the Society, please write to:

The Kalamalka New Writers Society
7000 College Way
Vernon, B.C. V1B 2N5